I Was Not Born a Sad Poet

I dedicate this book to my grandson who died early without me setting my eyes on him. His heart beats quietly in mine still.

I Was Not Born A Sad Poet

Loraine Masiya Mponela

published by Kindle Direct Publishing 2022

copy-edited by Lou Sarabadzic

published with the assistance of Counterpoints Arts

ISBN: 9798356662959

Contents

"I met Loraine many years ago at Coventry Peace House, she had organised a legal advice session where I was the guest speaker. What impressed me about Loraine was the ability to bring so many people together at the worst end of horrendous immigration law, giving them both hope and food. Neither should be underestimated nor should anyone underestimate Loraine, who has become a stand out go-to speaker to raise voices of the unheard."

Salman Mirza

About the author

Loraine Masiya Mponela is a Malawian-born mother, warrior, public speaker, writer and poet. Loraine is ex-chair for Coventry Asylum and Refugee Action Group (CARAG, 2018-2022). She is also one of the co-chairs for the Status Now 4 All network, which campaigns for Indefinite Leave to Remain for anyone who needs it in the UK.

As an activist, Loraine champions the lives of asylum seekers, as well as undocumented and marginalised people in the UK. Loraine has been described by others as an absolute textbook role model as to how to speak out and organise. She was recognised as Everyday Hero in 2020 and a modern day Lady Godiva in 2021 in Coventry, England where she now lives. She has been widely published, including in *Refugee Survey Quarterly* and *The Refugee Journalism Project*.

To visit her blog, go to: www.noaudienceloraine.co.uk.

Copy-editor's note

Above all, I want to thank Loraine Masiya Mponela for trusting me with her poems. For discussing words, images, sounds, rhythm, in a space that was full of emotions and painful memories.

To discover Loraine's poems is to learn new songs. Songs of hope, resistance, faith, grief, love, struggle, and so much more.

These words are here to stay. To ask difficult questions. To talk about silenced experiences. To express joy and anguish and everything in between. To show things for what they are.

Our society is not only unfair. It is extremely violent. Forcing so many people into despair and loneliness.

> "*knock knock knock*
>
> knuckles hitting a wall
>
> there is no door to this house
>
> I scream for attention
>
> just my echo thrown back at me"

I Shall Keep Knocking until the Door Opens

A voice echoing against a wall. A voice trying to reach out *From the Glass Bottle*.

But here's a voice fighting for others, too. A voice that knows so much about transmission. *Four-Generation Warriors*. Passing on the baton as wisdom is passed on. So often, it is also a tribute:

> "I am glad to say, I now wear your crown with pride
> nursing the oppressed and lifting the weak
> not from my breast but from my voice, Mama"

Mama

In the abecedarian poem *How to Walk with Me*, the reader is made aware that "Indifference is not an option". And it can't be an option in a world of racist immigration laws:

> "Questions shall be answered
> Revisited at the end, for now let's walk
> Soon we shall celebrate
> Through all the barricades of systematic abuse"

So for now, let's walk.

For now, let's read.

Lou Sarabadzic

Lou Sarabadzic is a French-born writer and translator based in England. For more information about her work, visit www.lousarabadzic.com

Foreword

Words...

Words are powerful. They have the power to build. They have the power to destroy.

When Loraine shared that finally her words were being printed and published, I felt so much excitement. I knew that, as readers, we were about to embark on a visceral journey. I know Loraine via our various projects to do with supporting refugees and asylum seekers. I will not go into the details of the projects, nor the rights and wrongs of the system. We will get a glimpse of that in this book.

Loraine is somebody's child. A granddaughter to her grandmother, a grandmother who devotedly raised her. Loraine is mother to a son she lovingly birthed into this world and committed to. She is a sister to many, an advocate for those who have been silenced. Loraine is a warrior, she's a woman with red blood running through her veins, that means when cut, she bleeds. Like you and me, she has feelings. Loraine is a WARRIOR who does not give up. She is not a label, she is not her circumstances.

She loves, she laughs, she executes. Period!

It's a joy and honour to write a foreword for *I Was Not Born a Sad Poet*. I know that each and every word in this book is coming from deep within. It's reality, not fiction. There's something about Loraine's writing that makes me laugh at pain, as if she's told the wildest joke I've ever heard. Her poems give us, readers, a glimpse of frozen moments in Loraine's life. These poems are the literal version of what they call lived experience, an attempt to capture or bottle one's moments in time.

Moments of *Joy*, moments of *Sleep,* moments when the system makes decisions that are so inhumane that one feels the need to write to make sense of one's life, in order to survive.

Loraine and I have worked together on a number of projects. *I Was Not Born a Sad Poet* strikes a chord. It carries a trunk full of what I've witnessed Loraine go through over the years, in her multiple roles as CARAG Chairperson, Sister, Advocate, Mother, Counsellor, Asylum Seeker, the list is endless. I've often asked Loraine, *how do you do it?*

Loraine always answers, "*you got to do, what you got to do.*"

If you ask me what picture comes to my mind when I think of Loraine, I see her smiling. Loraine is not a sad poet.

This book is a call to you and I as readers to stop, transport our heart, body, mind, soul, spirit to a MOMENT in time.

The moment when Bukhary Afifi Ahmad died in an asylum hostel all by himself.

In *The Limbo Land*, you will experience a fleeting taste of the pain, hopelessness that one experiences in a frozen state of being. In Limbo.

In *Still I Am Limitless*, you will encounter a roaring lioness, declaring strengths and resilience.

We are living in a fast paced, fast changing world, the majority of the changes are negative. We have migrants and asylum seekers crossing borders everyday. Beyond the labels Refugee, Asylum Seeker, Migrant, they are somebody's child. When we look closely, they are YOU, they are ME.

My closing remark is, these are not poems to woo. This is a call from one full-blooded human to another full-blooded human. It's a call to action.

What are we going to do about it?!

Laura Nyahuye

Laura Nyahuye is a creative visionary born and raised in Zimbabwe, and based in Coventry, UK. Heavily influenced by her African heritage, Laura's creative practice spans spoken word, poetry, a palette of textures. She is also the founder and Creative Director of Maokwo, an organisation using art as a form of activism to bring about positive change.

Introduction

I read Loraine's poems on the day my colleagues told me they called 24 legal aid solicitors to refer refugees and migrants needing legal advice and who qualify for legal aid. Still, they could not find anyone able to take on new clients. This is terrifying for the people concerned and another slap across the face of our democracy and the rule of law, induced by the immigration system framed through the hostile environment ideology of enforcement, racism and xenophobia.

The list of egregious violations of human dignity and fundamental rights at the heart of this hostile ideology is terrifying. The scale and depth of dehumanisation resulting from this ideology are often unimaginable for people without direct experience of it. And for those of us who do, it can be hard to muster and sustain the energy needed to resist the soul-destroying despair and the reality of survival for those subjected to abuse and hostility by the state, public services, media and people around us.

And then I read Loraine's *Ode to Hope*:

> "it is you, Hope
> that enables us to access legal aid
> so our words and experiences are never twisted
> or our ignorance of the system
> is never taken advantage of"

This, and other poems in the making of the sad poet Loraine, are a powerful reminder that hope is not a belief that everything will be fine. It is essential to fuel survival and resistance.

Loraine is a poet. She is also a community organiser and a campaigner who fought for and supported hundreds of other people while being subjected to the hostile environment immigration system for more than a decade.

It is where Loraine's power comes from. Power to confront and name her sadness and pain. Power to feel compassion for herself and others. Power to be joyful. Power to imagine and to speak out.

In 2016, Rebecca Solnit wrote, "Our opponents would love you to believe that it's hopeless, that you have no power, that there's no reason to act, that you can't win. Hope is a gift you don't have to surrender, a power you don't have to throw away."[1]

In *How to Walk with Me*, Loraine tells us about the power we all have, and should not throw away – the power to be with Loraine and sad, hopeful and powerful poets hiding in all of us:

> "Accept me as I am
>
> Be with me in my struggles

---

[1] *'Hope is an embrace of the unknown': Rebecca Solnit on living in dark times*, 15/07/16. https://bit.ly/3C7Vg3t. Last accessed on 04/10/22.

Converse with me, I am human

Diligently and with dignity engage with me"

Dr Zrinka Bralo

Zrinka Bralo has been the CEO of Migrants Organise since 2001. Migrants Organise is an award-winning grassroots platform where migrants and refugees organise together for dignity and justice for all. Zrinka is a refugee from Sarajevo, where she was a journalist and where she worked during the siege of Sarajevo in the 90's. For her work for migrants' justice she was awarded the '2011 Voices of Courage Award' by the Women's Refugee Commission in New York. Zrinka holds an MSc in Media and Communications from London School of Economics and in 2022 was awarded an Honorary Doctorate from Exeter University.

Waiting on God

I wait on You   God

to do what You have repeatedly done in the past

taking me from glory to glory

mercy to compassion

to make me meld with all Your creation

I wait on You   God   to lead the way

not my own way as it is usually filled with selfish desires

I need your way Lord

Your way includes everybody

and just make me be one with all

Creator of heaven and earth

why do I think I am waiting on You?

who pumps blood in my heart at night

and makes the blood course in my veins and arteries

when I am in deep sleep unaware of anything?

who walks in my dreams

foretelling the past and the future

celebrating and crying sometimes all in one dream

who is this mystery that has stayed with me

directing and pointing all the time

is that you God?

the Redeemer, Restorer and Healer,

make me realise my power

and with it work towards a destiny of my choice and say

I receive it

I activate it

Hallelujah!

make me soar above mountains of challenges

of anger and hate and petty behaviours

of self-conceit and pride

and make me be the one who realises

that all along I have been one with You and

You one with me

always.

Four-Generation Warriors

I did not get to see my great grandmother

but her nose is on my face

her smile written on my lips

I never saw her face

warriors who do not give up

I was told she died at a young age

crushed by womanhood

giving birth

toiling in the fields

raising a family

warriors who do not give up

I did not see my great grandmother

yet I walk her footsteps

finding locked gates everywhere

humanity's tradition having been replaced with laws

that becry my racial stamp

reminding me that she died young

from a life of constant struggle

I can imagine my great grandmother

breathing her last

thinking about the children

the two young girls of ten and six years

warriors who do not give up

I saw my grandmother

her face etched with suffering

and the worry of many foremothers

her back arched from the physical burdens

and the furrows on her face

from the emotional load

she has been carrying since she was ten

I can see my grandmother

her old body, a mirror of mine

sturdy and strong, ready to face the fight

the fight she started when she was ten

she looks at us with her face stern

wondering if we can carry the baton

and hand it over to the next generation

a generation whose struggle is not known

and whose challenges can not be estimated

but a generation that shall overcome

like she and hers did

and then pass on the baton too

when the time is right

warriors who do not give up

I can see my mother

weary from carrying six pregnancies

including twins

with her body limp

saying: I have given my all

now is the time to take your place

and fight a woman's warrior fight

never giving up

but realise that in your veins

runs the blood of women

warriors who do not give up

without giving a good fight

so here I am.

Ode to Hope

Hope

you moisten my eyes every morning

and embrace me in a loving hold

without a word being said

you give me my new day

later

you give me food and enough for everyone

pangs of hunger completely forgotten

you remind me of who I am

and deliver the diet that I need

Hope

you never wince or whine, like a veritable companion

you give without taking, reminding me of your power

which rests in silence

which rests in resilience

without you

I imagine a longing for a hot cuppa tea

or a roast Sunday dinner

for not having anything to hold on to

you give me more than enough

you give me more than a laugh

it is you, Hope

who has provided us a home, our own space with heating

and a hot shower, uncontrolled access to the kitchen and garden

a place to rest and relax for the night

a place to nestle and nurse our dreams

Hope

you are our happiness, you are the reason

no one lived in despair and destitution

no one lived in graveyards for lack of home

no one died under the bridge for lack of food

with full love

you buy us clothes to cover our scars for winter and summer

you let us have our own washing machines and dryers

to silence those who only know how to judge us

for being clean

imagine

no one having frozen feet

frozen fingers crawling in snow

for wearing torn shoes

torn socks and no gloves

it is you, Hope

that enables us to access legal aid

so our words and experiences are never twisted

or our ignorance of the system

is never taken advantage of

imagine everyone getting justice

although delayed, a choice to choose how to live

imagine better treatment for everyone

addressing power imbalances, not bullying

but building trust instead

Hope

you safeguard our right to work

and access to benefit, we do not lack

only in abundance we swim together

finding a common ground and thrive together

I imagine

ruthless employers or so-called husbands or wives

dishing us daily abuses

because of their control over us

but Hope, you give us an escape route

none without mental capacity

will have to live on their own

and end up being burned to death

forgotten in the hustle and bustle of life

Hope, you safeguard our mental state

I imagine

the laughter, love, and luxury

the joy, happiness, and life

as you live with us, Hope, and a gentle reminder that says:

insanity will no longer be our portion

Hope

you open the gate to the university

so our children are not traumatised

by rampant hate, prejudice, segregation, and racism

better life is guaranteed with you, Hope, free of all -isms

with you by my side

I imagine an asylum child

becoming a surgeon in Covid wards

becoming a psychologist for Covid patients

and far much more

Hope

I trust you

one day you shall hand out travel passports

cut out all the chains from their roots

and give me wings

so I can soar high like an eagle again

I imagine meeting friends

across ponds and oceans

exploring the world, making a difference

and changing lives in my own little ways

Hope

like everybody else you take your time

but my faith gives birth to your new offspring

and so my resolve is ever renewed

with you Hope

there is no place for unfulfilled dreams

and delayed promises, all prayers are answered

only happiness fills my past

only happiness fills my paths

I would rather lose it all

but still have you, Hope, by my side

my never complaining companion,

Hope.

From the Glass Bottle

have you ever been in a bottle

a colourless bottle

with a tightly closed top?

you can see the flowers and trees

but can't smell the roses

you are not allowed.

you can see the bees and insects

but can't feel them on your skin

they are not allowed.

you can see the cars drive past

but in muffled sounds.

you exist and you don't.

you touch but nothing touches you

sometimes you want to escape

this prison with open walls

where I wear a tag

that says, I can't get a job

a life, a relationship, or just be happy

because the bottle has rules.

am I going mad, thinking the trees lie

when they sway to an invisible breeze

playing with my mind?

these soundless birds hoping from branch to branch

acting out a silent recital of my death

which is being in a bottle with a top

tightly closed.

I am not being treated humanely

for the biggest crime of needing help

and therefore confined to a bottle

where I see everything but never touch.

oh that juicy job flying by

that course I could do

that meal in a restaurant

all too good for the one

whose life is a bottle.

I am shouting, screaming for attention, tears streaming

hitting the bottle walls with my fist

but no one hears me

and I can't hear anyone

the pain to know

that outside this glass bottle

there is a life,

a normal life.

will I ever live again?

can somebody talk to me?

please somebody break the glass bottle

I need to breathe fresh air too

like every other human being.

In My Sleep

every night I get called to a place

of love and solitude,

I meet with all my heroes and sheroes.

it's a place of quiet and peace

in my sleep.

oh, who goes there?

is it you Mandela,

do you still dare advise me in your gravelly voice

to love my enemy as I love myself?

to let bygones be bygones?

who is this passing by, Mother Teresa?

are your gnarled hands impervious

to the wounds you dress

bandaging falling limbs from leprosy

and never shedding a tear

or covering your nose

from the putrid smell

of decaying flesh around you?

yes, Dr Kamuzu Banda,

do you still sing our national anthem

Chiuta Mtumbike Malawi, mumupe mutende

and scream *Kwacha!*

as if it's your praise song

or have you mended your mean ways?

Cassius Clay, still sting like a bee

and fly like a butterfly?

are your fists all rolled up now

as symbols of peace?

hey King Shaka, the African Emperor!

demonised for your skills

by those that understood you

not.

yes, there is a place I go every night

to commune with my African ancestors

heroes, sheroes who we know are gone

in this dimension and life

yet in my sleep…

Mama

I nursed from your breast when I was just a baby

you continued to feed me when I was a toddler

you continued to feed me even more as a youth

even in death, you feed me still, Mama

you shared your knowledge and life skills

when I became an adult

I got to know what it means to love completely

I got nothing else in me, Mama

you did the same for your grandson

always giving

always taking nothing back, Mama

you are a star

feeding my thoughts and emotions all the time

feeding me even now that you are not here

even in death, you feed me still, Mama

with twenty-two years today gone but still

I feel you close-by in my dreams

I feel you in my troubled times

I am always engulfed by your love and care, Mama

you mothered so many

who were not your offspring

you defined community, defied patriarchy

even in death, you feed me still, Mama

I am glad to say, I now wear your crown with pride

nursing the oppressed and lifting the weak

not from my breast but from my voice, Mama

soon, when my time comes to join you

in the deathless kingdom

I surely should have a good report

about how you nursed me to nurse others

and that your tradition continues

on people and lands

we both shall never physically know, Mama.

My Grandson

our uteruses are on fire

our eyes burning from dry tears

our wombs crushed

as you lie in the cooler

taking your shortest route.

what do we do now

when our little flower

without formal goodbyes

vanishes?

we are tired of pain

no words can quantify

our breath is running away

life feels meaningless.

your dad waited

behind the labour ward windows

later moved near to the theatre

so he could remember your first cry.

your mother

the one whose womb

you chose

is still lying on her back

waiting in agony.

with bags full of clothes and toys

my hands still holding on

to your little shoes.

our hope lies in knowing

that you are with the Lord

smiling at us till we join you

we will always love you.

I Was Not Born a Sad Poet

I was not born sad

nobody is, that would be mad

I am a sad poet because of the circumstances

that life's deal which put me on the edge

I live on the edge of society, of the law

not because I want it

I am a rebel with a cause filled with another purpose

and sometimes I am sad

sad for decisions not being made in time

sad for years of waiting

sad for years of not knowing what

sad for living on charity when I have hands

and the brains to fend for myself

sad for many others like me who take their own lives

because of the gloom in their eyes

I could be a happy poet

happy to be alive

happy for health and sunshine

but someone has switched off the lights

I can't see the sun

nor hear the flying birds

as I listen to my thumping heart

that exists in the fear and sadness

of a poor mental health state

of seven years of inactivity and degeneration

I look sad

because my sadness is no longer inside

it has become my logo

the cauldron where poems and thoughts are churned

to calm my trembling spirit

which has been denied of sleep and restfulness

in both day and night

I am sad I have to fight

for a morsel of food

I am sad I have to fight

for an audience with important people

who control my life and make decisions

as to who I am

and who I can be

I am a sad poet but I could be a happy poet

I am sad now but not always

I am more than that

I am human, with a million emotions

for now pulsating under the banner of sadness

because of the decaying mental health

of me and my friends

helping them become better

and not sad

will help me to become better

and not sad.

The Limbo Land

in limbo land of asylum seeker I dwell,

my beloved landlord; the Home Office

holds my key to work office

day after day for seven years I wait

they haven't forgotten me

they call me when they wish

control me like a marionette

dancing to swooshing sounds of letters

dropped through the door

and to texts telling me to report

or do something else

I am like a baby they don't want,

called far too young to do errands

never brought to the dining table nor celebrated

the key of my coming of age

being held tightly in their hands

my breath is controlled

by the footsteps outside my room

waiting for my name to be called

for a transition to

I don't know where

I spend too much time in my room

afraid that outside I will betray my fears

and let everyone see my silent tears

I have a life but it's not mine,

It's controlled by an amorphous office

that decides what I do or do not do

I am not shackled but my mind is

locked in the eternal battle

of when will this nightmare end

I wonder

which shall come first

the loss of my breath

or that of my mind

it's so hard living in limbo land.

I Am Enough

I was told I was only good for nothing

that was a lie.

I was told as a woman I can't stand up and speak

I can't shine by being truly who I am

that was a lie.

I was told I was only good for raising children

that education was a waste of time

that was a lie.

I was told as an asylum seeker I should zip it

and be grateful even when it hurts

that was a lie.

I then told myself something different

I

am worthy

I

am deserving

I

am enough

that was no lie.

I am enough

I was born great

I deserve all the best things in life

I am as good as anybody

if not better

I will open my mouth as wide as hell

and for as long as I live

this list is not exhaustive

because I am not done yet

I listen to myself and not others.

the universe is big enough for one like me

making no excuses

just cruising

with oxygen in my lungs

carrying me higher and higher

under the wings of love and compassion

from He who created the earth and the moon.

if I am not enough so is the moon

and the stars and the sun

and remember the silent trees

exchanging carbon dioxide for oxygen

with no drama or questions

just doing their thing

just like me

I am enough.

Do Not Let Bukhary Be Forgotten!

today, 18th July 2021

is another dark day

another death in asylum hotel

another body without a soul

Bukhary Afifi Ahmad

is no more.

a young Sudanese asylum seeker

so far away from home

confronted by a hostile system

living in poor conditions and neglect

suffering from the never ceasing trauma

of war, death and destruction.

a man who has never known peace

concerns were raised but ignored

it becomes too much

echoes of loneliness change

to echoes of pain.

now we are left with questions.

why Bukhary, why?

without disclosing even to one friend?

how many emergency demonstrations are enough

to stop these deaths?

do we wait for them to reach that threshold

and regroup again and say why?

do not let Bukhary be forgotten

for in the system are many Bukharys.

Ode to Joy

oh Joy, where do you come from

emanating with a fresh fragrance of dancing flowers

and a cool breeze

you lift my wings and dry my tears

without saying a word

I want to dedicate this ode to you

and call you by name in jubilation

for your enduring power that makes me

see day after day

sometimes under a blue mood

the spectra of Covid-19 has decimated love

filled us with fear and trepidation

but we still live and need you, Joy

now more than ever

we invite you to invade our lives

and take us prisoner for ever and ever

you are welcome in my life, Joy

bring your true companion, happiness

next time you come

I treasure you for all eternity

you take not my blood or demand my money

I summon you anytime but you are not my slave

you are a trusty friend

you don't chide me for being down

waiting for my foul mood to wash away

and taking back your place quietly

as if nothing had happened

you remind me of who I am

a lone wanderer, who laughed as a child

for no reason but that you enveloped me completely

and gave me my identity

life has taught me grief and sadness

yet you don't fight them

you wait your turn like a polite child

and wrap your arms around me

gently whispering: it shall be alright

I treasure you, your power creeping silently

your energy, invisible

but the cause of my smile and the light fluttering of my heart

like one who has glimpsed their lover passing by

to a place of stolen rendezvous

you give bountifully and take nothing in return

I have never known such satisfaction

from just the joy of being human

and this is my little ode to you

Joy, thou shall not leave me.

Still I Am Limitless

I am everything

I am the wind blowing but unseen

I am the sunlight, shining on wilting souls

I am a force of nature full of life

I am a fearless public speaker

climbing barbed wires

reaching for the podium

torn clothes are my trademark

a symbol of my struggle

to becoming limitless

I am an autodidact poet

performing distressing stories

in open mics

still I am limitless

I am a double-barreled mother

to my own and then more

holding on to the dying child

Still I am limitless

I am a fighter

climbing steps to the thirteenth floor

standing tall barefoot

catching insults

still I am limitless

I am a woman

among feminist women

trying to squeeze my chair

in the circle

still I am limitless

still I am limitless

still I am limitless

Luromo Peninsula

majestic landmark

of my ancestors

trodden for a millennia

full of mysterious ghosts

alive and dead

fountain of youth

for trees and animals

all drink from your bounty

of wild fruits and rolling hills

I call you my home

blessed with unique plants

lakes with unique fish

nurturing the young and old

in your water gold

you are older than these mountains

and these rivers that daily caress

your undulating cheeks

whispering in a language unknown

all sing praises of your beauty and wealth

I hold you in my chest

like a little child

you have given me life

if I were to sleep and never wake

I would like to lie in your blossom

forever and ever.

My Dad Is Waiting to Welcome Me

early in life I had a lesson

death came into my family

and reminded us of its close

proximity to humankind

that can't be resisted, dodged or postponed.

my dad's life was cut short

I was left orphaned

and now dad rests

in divine power and eternally

in our Father's kingdom.

I know my father

he waits for me in heaven

with his long warm hands

and tears in his eyes

precursing a flood of joy

of our meeting.

his calming smile shall welcome me

our love will shine

we shall hold hands in an eternal embrace

never to be separated even for a moment.

Death of a Hero

For Penny Walker (1950-2021)

Penny Walker had a house

a tranquil place filled with love and care

but now she made it ours too.

Penny gave us her house

protecting us all

taking away our homeless shame

and clothing us with a name home.

our house, the one that Penny gave us

is a peace garden, where all plants grow

just like us, the human exotic plants

call this place home.

there is a Zimbabwean cabbage

rhubarb that endures all weather all year round

it never changes, green peace and love all year round

never dying, like Penny's love.

Penny, you are gone

but in your place stands a garden of peace

with creeping strawberries ready

to be picked and eaten.

creeping beans ready to harvest

every fruit and plant so special

like the touch of your warm hands.

these standing little plants

giving birth to sweet fruits

pregnant with aroma that even babies can pick

and caress as they often do

are a symbol of how accessible you were.

Penny, your love grows

just like the cherry and big tomatoes

growing side by side with sunflower

yellow candle flames bringing light

in a colourful spectacle

like the love you still exude.

Penny, you left us a food bank house.

with three apple trees standing majestically

two at the back and another in front

which bear green and red apples

in a mix of sweet yet sour

that falls freely on the ground

just like your tears at the sight of the homeless.

Penny, you left us a house that we now share

with many visitors including the birds

birds still making their presence felt

in loud songs and the mess on our table

as if they were saying: “like Penny, we were here.”

you left us a sanctuary

you gave us a calming house.

calming distressed children

a garden of yellow roses, white flowers

that shine as bright at night as the full moon

where I sit and at times play football or dance

to my tribal healing songs.

and I will remember you always when I sit

in this, my favourite hotspot

free from shade of heavenly bound trees

where I walk barefoot

connecting my body with nature, grounding

feeling the warmth from under my feet.

in the peace garden

a place where we can rest

from the sun's penetrating rays

a place where we can light open fires

feeling the warmth penetrating from the top of my head to my longest foot

I burn my struggles and calm my mind.

at this moment I think of you, Penny

gone and yet here

enveloping me in the four walls of my room

your spirit caressing every window

calming me to sleep

in a place that we call our house

and the place I simply call home.

Rest In Power

Penny Walker.

How to Walk with Me

Accept me as I am

Be with me in my struggles

Converse with me, I am human

Diligently and with dignity engage with me

Every passing minute, we lose

Focus when we engage in hate

Greet me and light my spirit

Human I am and so are you

Indifference is not an option

Just like a beating heart, think not of stopping

Kill the state of knowing, be curious instead

Let me hold your hand and walk with me

My journey finishes when all are free

Nobody left behind

Only holding each other's hands

Pity is not to be served now - let's walk

Questions shall be answered

Revisited at the end, for now let's walk

Soon we shall celebrate

Through all the barricades of systematic abuse

Until the end, this walk is all we have

Victory or life, our lives are on the line

Who really wants to live like this e-

Xamined and inspected every day when reporting

You would not know it unless you walk with me, so

Zero down with me and hold my hand, let's walk.

You Have Robbed Me of My Midlife

I remember.

14th September 2008 when I left home

I was standing at Lilongwe International Airport

in the departures lounge, waving at my children

feeling the warmth from my nieces and cousins' gestures.

yes I remember.

the September sun was hot,

making it the hottest time of that year

grass was almost dry, seen from the aeroplane's window

cattle resting under mango trees.

I remember

I had just turned thirty-four

my head filled with dreams, hopes and aspirations

I could see the life I was crafting

through sheer hard work and study

for myself, my family and friends.

yes I remember

all the dreams

of a good and fulfilling life

as a single mother of a teenage boy.

I remember

15th September 2008

arriving at London Heathrow

it was freezing, I was cold and

experienced snow for the first time that year.

now I realise

close to fifty I am

my life upside down, dreams shattered

prison like, worse than the poverty

this is what my life is now.

now I am acutely aware that I have,

no family

no home

no hope.

is it a curse? I have asked myself.

you have robbed me of my midlife.

now I realise

I am a different person

withdrawn

lacking in confidence

prone to stress and worry.

now I know

my midlife came flying past me

how can thirteen years change one's life so?

not even in my wildest dream

could I conjure such a nightmare.

now I don't even know

where I will be in a year or

what I will be doing

what I will become.

now it's clear

my life is not my own.

I Shall Keep Knocking until the Door Opens

knock knock knock

knuckles hitting a wall

there is no door to this house

I scream for attention

just my echo thrown back at me

a house would bring a sense of safety

I could live here just like everyone else

and choose to take matters into my own hands

I know what I deserve

did dig dig

dead fingers

I am making a hole so I can let myself in

no matter how strongly l dig

it's as though I am being welcomed by a hard rock

only my tears leave a trace on the concrete

once,

fighting for civil and economic rights

Dr MLK on 28th August 1963 said

we cannot walk alone.

today, 16th June 2021

the journey to creating a fairer, freer world is still alive

battling new immigration plans

the fight to exercise our rights, refugees' rights

*we cannot walk alon*e.

knock knock knock

there is no door to this house

to friends we have lost, never to be forgotten

to restore what's lost, reclaim our power

we must walk together because

our freedom is your freedom

knock knock knock

there is no door to this house

though knuckles bleed and oh it hurts

knocking is now more than a choice

it is my lifeline.

and I can see my bleeding bony bones

bony fingers

I watch my blood flowing from my elbows

I shall keep knocking

till these hands are just stumps

I shall keep knocking until the door opens

knock knock knock.

Lambs of Sacrifice

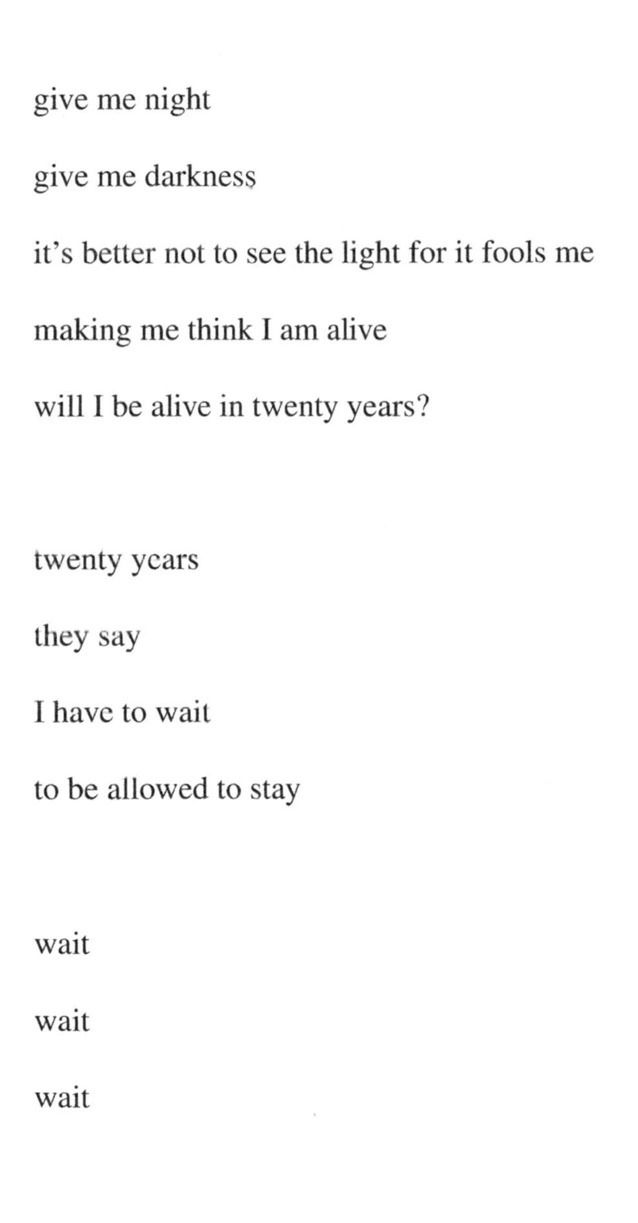

give me night

give me darkness

it's better not to see the light for it fools me

making me think I am alive

will I be alive in twenty years?

twenty years

they say

I have to wait

to be allowed to stay

wait

wait

wait

all my dreams and hopes on hold

till I get twenty years older

then I can start living and breathing

what's worse, being alive and awake now

compared to being dead and asleep

only to be told wake up, now you can live

in the time interval of twenty years?

let me sleep and not wake up

and let all my dreams rush to the sea

for awake is worse than asleep

and death is a better friend

who in their right minds can wait for twenty years

to be called human

after such a long time being denied everything human

will I still remember how?

bring death if you can

be swift

puncture my veins

make deep scars

get every artery bleeding

let the blood flow

it shall soon ebb and stop just like my weak heart

that is losing the will to live

it makes no difference

for many years now

I have watched my soul leaving

dripping

from my bone marrow

painting red the soil where I stand

in the shape of the feet

still planted on the ground

a reminder of my being tied to a spot

I am tied to a stake, with silent crowds watching

ready to be burnt in the solemn sacrifice

to underscore a cruel policy

set by people

who use me for their own ends to send a message

to those running for their lives

saying they are not welcome here

look at the ones we burn on the stake

even the fittest twenty-three-year-old Mustafa Dawood

who loved trekking mountains

could not survive, though he tried

like a bag of cement Mustafa's body came down flying

from the rooftop killed for working illegally

running away from a battalion of immigration officers

who raided his car wash workplace

I feel Mustafa's body falling with a thud, many bones broken

I read his pained mother's plea at his inquest

"my son was not a thief or a murderer but he died like one"

I have become the lamb of sacrifice

not tied to a cross

but to documents and policies

those on the cross had it easy

their deaths were swift

I wait for a file with my life

sequestered somewhere in an office cabinet

it shall be handed back to me after twenty years

twenty years!

who knows twenty years?

in twenty years, a child born becomes a grown up

married and having children

but twenty years of my life will have been taken away

I can't believe it's happening

I can only start my life again

in twenty years.

Not Making Waves

I live in the middle

my mouth wearing half a smile and half a snarl

my eyes teary with instant mirth or instant cry

my face a contortion of aches and cheerfulness

so much has happened

and yet so much to come

living in the unknown

I live in the middle of adversity and happiness

just like the country I live in, so rich

and yet I, so poor

I am a contrasting rainbow of pain and laughter

I am facing a quick approaching middle age

with nothing to show

I wake up in the middle of the night to listen to silence

it is a sound of peace, far closer to death than life

after all I live comfortably between life and death

I am drawn closer to the death and life daily

by the news that talk about my fate

without my involvement

I am a prisoner who is not jailed

boundless but still not free

I am caught in my sad thoughts

of misery and happiness

next time you ask me how I am

my answer shall be, “I am in the middle!”

that is where I am

neither here nor there,

just existing and not making waves.

Acknowledgements

I am grateful for the sterling work executed by my editors who have worked hard on this project. Special thanks to Lou Sarabadzic, who worked tirelessly for copy editing the poems, Tom Green and Counterpoints Arts for making sure my poems get published.

I am thankful to my entire family for their prayers, my brother Francis, my son Comfort, my sisters Wezi and Donias and their families who always support me, even on the toughest days. My thoughts are also going to the giants whose shoulders I stand on, my maternal grandmother, my mother and brother Robert Vachalo Mponela. May their souls continue to rest in peace.

My heartfelt thanks to Coventry Asylum and Refugee Action Group (CARAG) for welcoming me and allowing me to be part of their journey. I wish to thank Coventry Peace House too for being a brave space and always offering shelter.

My gratitude would not be enough without mentioning Laura Nyahuye from Maokwo Arts who supports me in so many ways in my writing journey. Thanks should also go to the following: all Coventry Activists for always showing up in the streets; Joan Proctor "the queen mother" and her sister Bernice, for encouraging me to stay strong over the years; the entire UK migration sector for standing with me and those like me; Malawi Leeds Association and Daughters of Nyasa

Coventry for their friendship; my lil sister from another mother Molly Mpando, for holding my hand; Linda Mlombwa, I love you sis; all the groups I am part of in Leeds, Birmingham and Coventry; Amanda Sebestyen and all my close friends, thank you for the part you play in my life.

I am also grateful for the support of my friends and readers on Zoom, WhatsApp, Facebook, Twitter and YouTube who have said they love my poems and have encouraged me to publish them. And thank you to all the online poetry groups and open mics for cheering me on. Thanks to Room 204 and Writing West Midlands for their insights, and to Writers At Play for accepting me and being part of the family. Thank you to The Poetry Business for their bursary spaces to their writing sessions. Last but not least, deep thanks to all my mentors including but not limited to Minda Burgos-Lukes, Salman Mirza, Zrinka Bralo, Dr Rhetta Moran and others.

Thank you all for believing in what I write and love.

Earlier versions of the poems included in this book have previously appeared in the following publications, or been shared on the following platforms:

From the Glass Bottle has been published in the book *Seeking Asylum and Mental Health: A Practical Guide for Professionals,* edited by Chris Maloney, Julia Nelki, Alison Summers, Cambridge University Press, 2022.

Luromo Peninsula was first published by *Legacy Poetry* in an anthology by my international creative writing group, Writers At Play, a project run by *Legacy Poetry & Equal Arts* in 2021.

Ode to Hope was part of the Coventry Methodist Hall project under the theme Hope, Faith and Love in 2021.

It is also important to mention what inspired some of these poems:

I Am Enough was created during a writing workshop, thanks to a "*That was a lie*" prompt at the Writing For Wellness For Women workshop that took place in September 2021, facilitated by Kim B. Miller, Poet Laureate of Prince William County, VA.

Do Not Let Bukhary Be Forgotten! is based on and was inspired by an email from the *Migration Struggles* Google group sent in July 2021.

Not Making Waves was inspired by Barbara Crooker's poem *In the Middle* through an online workshop run by Word Artist Michelle Berberet.

In *I Shall Keep Knocking until the Door Opens,* the phrase "we cannot walk alone" is taken from one of Dr Martin Luther King's Speeches.

Printed in Great Britain
by Amazon